ALL JAZZED UP!
INTERMEDIATE PIANO SOLO

OZZY OSBOURNE

T0061429

Cover photo: Getty Images / Martin Philbey / Contributor

ISBN 978-1-4950-3066-6

HAL•LEONARD®
CORPORATION

7777 W. BLUEMOUND RD. P.O. BOX 13819 MILWAUKEE, WI 53213

Visit Hal Leonard Online at
www.halleonard.com

CRAZY TRAIN

Words and Music by OZZY OSBOURNE,
RANDY RHOADS and BOB DAISLEY

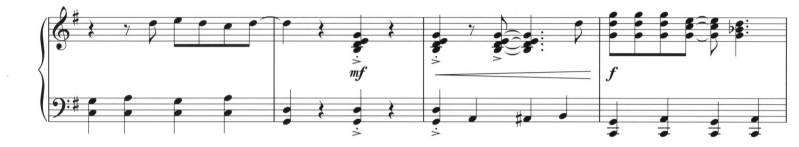

GOODBYE TO ROMANCE

Words and Music by JOHN OSBOURNE,
ROBERT DAISLEY and RANDY RHOADS

Moderate Bounce à la "I Love Lucy" ($\quad$ = 100)

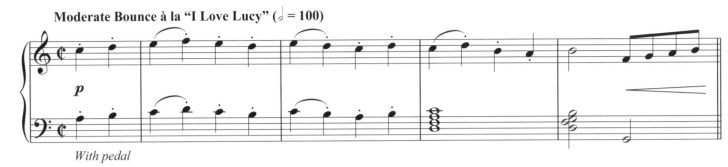

With pedal

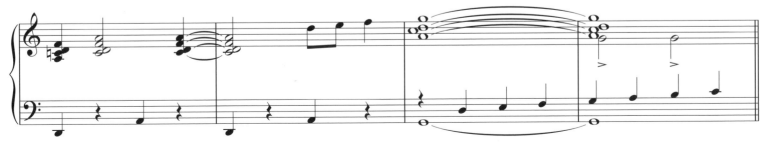

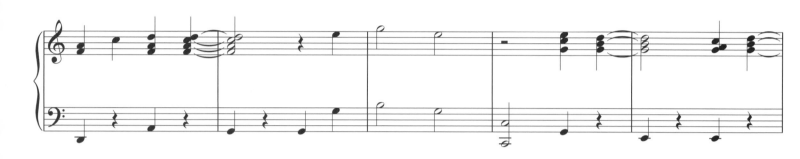

DREAMER

Words and Music by MARTI FREDERIKSEN,
OZZY OSBOURNE and MICK JONES

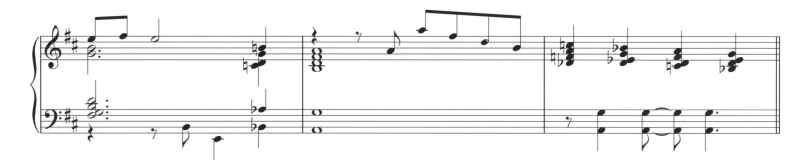

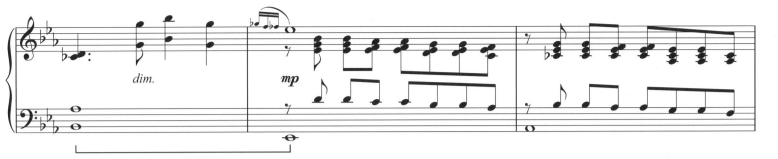

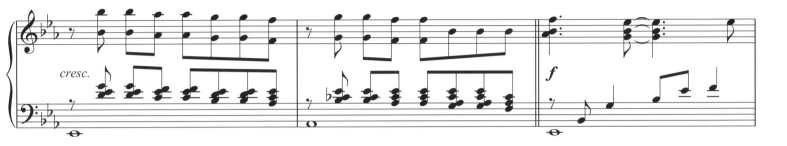

FLYING HIGH AGAIN

Words and Music by OZZY OSBOURNE,
RANDY RHOADS, BOB DAISLEY
and LEE KERSLAKE

Bright Swing (♩ = 160)

With pedal

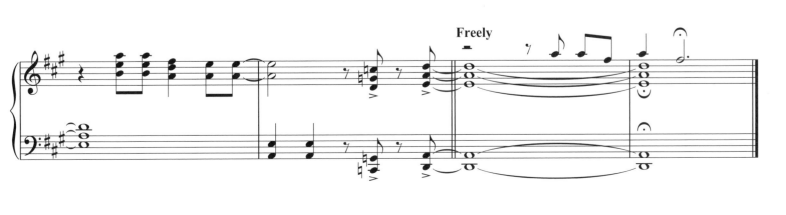

IRON MAN

Words and Music by FRANK IOMMI,
JOHN OSBOURNE, WILLIAM WARD
and TERENCE BUTLER

Jazz Waltz (♩ = 192)

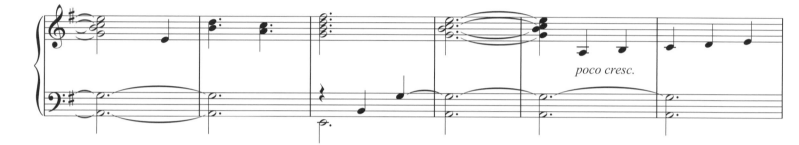

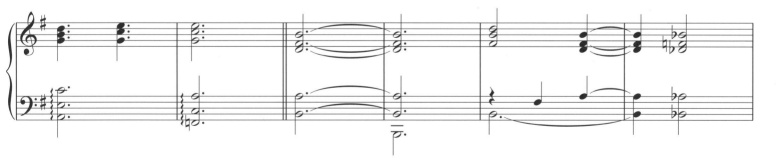

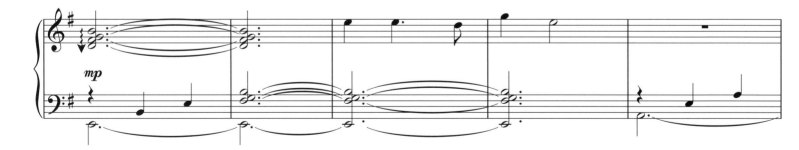

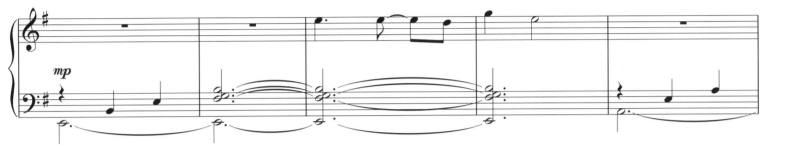

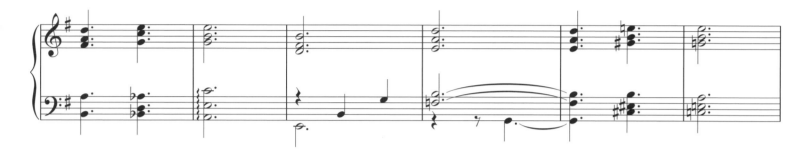

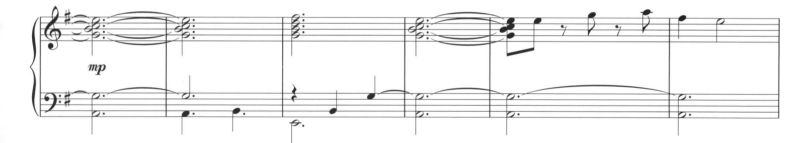

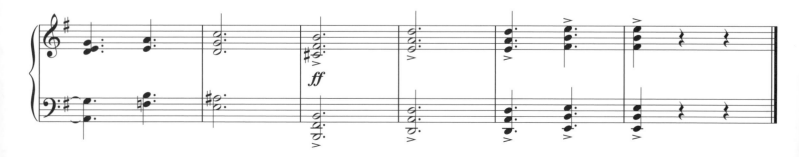

MAMA, I'M COMING HOME

Words and Music by OZZY OSBOURNE
and ZAKK WYLDE

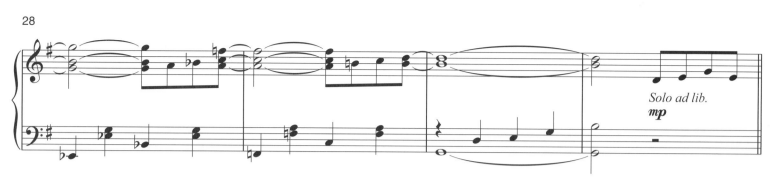

MR. CROWLEY

Words and Music by OZZY OSBOURNE,
RANDY RHOADS and BOB DAISLEY

Tango (♩ = 120)

With pedal

cresc. poco a poco

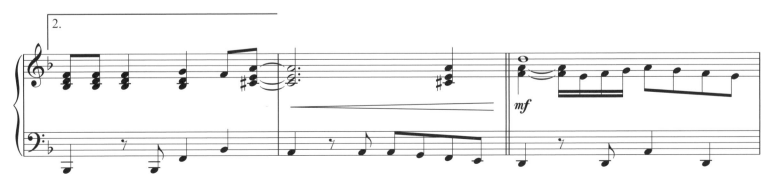

OVER THE MOUNTAIN

Words and Music by OZZY OSBOURNE,
RANDY RHOADS, BOB DAISLEY
and LEE KERSLAKE

Bright Swing (♩ = 152)

NO MORE TEARS

Words and Music by OZZY OSBOURNE,
ZAKK WYLDE and JOHN PURDELL

Moderately slow Salsa (♩ = 76)

With pedal

CODA

p

cresc. poco a poco

f

ff

PARANOID

Words and Music by ANTHONY IOMMI,
JOHN OSBOURNE, WILLIAM WARD
and TERENCE BUTLER

TIME AFTER TIME

Words and Music by OZZY OSBOURNE
and ZAKK WYLDE

PERRY MASON

Words and Music by OZZY OSBOURNE,
ZAKK WYLDE and JOHN PURDELL

Slowly and freely

With pedal

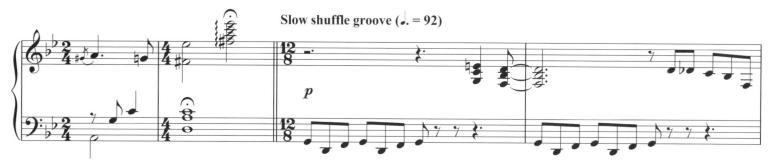

Slow shuffle groove (♩. = 92)